TOGETHER
WE CAN™

Celebrating the Power of a Team and a Dream.™

Compiled by Dan Zadra

Designed by Kobi Yamada and Steve Potter

COMPENDIUM™
INCORPORATED

live inspired.

ACKNOWLEDGEMENTS

These quotations were gathered lovingly but unscientifically over several years and/or contributed by many friends or acquaintances. Some arrived—and survived in our files—on scraps of paper and may therefore be imperfectly worded or attributed. To the authors, contributors and original sources, our thanks, and where appropriate, our apologies. —The Editors

WITH SPECIAL THANKS TO

Jason Aldrich, Gerry Baird, Jay Baird, Neil Beaton, Josie Bissett, Laura Boro, Melissa Carlson, M.H. Clark, Tiffany Parente Connors, Jim & Alyssa Darragh & Family, Rob Estes, Pamela Farrington, Michael & Leianne Flynn & Family, Sarah Forster, Dan Harrill, Michael J. Hedge, Liz Heinlein & Family, Renee Holmes, Jennifer Hurwitz, Heidi Jones, Sheila Kamuda, Michelle Kim, Carol Anne Kennedy, June Martin, David Miller, Carin Moore & Family, Moose, Josh Oakley, Jessica Phoenix & Tom DesLongchamp, Janet Potter & Family, Joanna Price, Heidi & José Rodriguez, Diane Roger, Alie Satterlee, Kirsten & Garrett Sessions, Andrea Shirley, Jason Starling, Brien Thompson, Helen Tsao, Anne Whiting, Heidi Yamada & Family, Justi & Tote Yamada & Family, Bob and Val Yamada, Kaz & Kristin Yamada & Family, Tai & Joy Yamada, Anne Zadra, August & Arline Zadra, and Gus & Rosie Zadra.

CREDITS

Compiled by Dan Zadra
Designed by Kobi Yamada and Steve Potter

ISBN: 978-1-888387-42-1

8th Printing.   Printed in China

CELEBRATING THE POWER OF A TEAM AND A DREAM.

EVERYONE
LEADS!

This book is loaded with good news and great quotations. If you're the leader of your organization, the good news is you're no longer alone. Tom Peters says it best: "The days of the Lone Ranger are over. Every organization worth its salt now realizes that every person in every position is called upon to lead, and lead well."

The truth is, our world has become too fast and too complicated for any one person to run the show. The role of today's leader is not to know everything or do everything. It's not to motivate people or threaten them. The role of today's leader is to help create a shared vision and to establish an atmosphere of trust, freedom and mutual respect.

If someone asked me to pick my top quote from this book, I'd have to pick two. The first one is only seven words:

"Ask your team—they know the answer." I once interviewed the leader of a 400,000-member educational organization. He was worried. The world was changing too fast; his organization's textbooks were outdated even before they were printed. "What will you do?" I asked him. He shrugged and smiled. "I don't have the answers," he said, "but I know 400,000 people who do." Nicely said.

My second favorite quote speaks for itself: "Hire the best. Pay them fairly. Communicate frequently. Provide meaningful challenges and rewards. Believe in them. Trust them. Get out of their way—they'll knock your socks off."

Together we can! Let these great quotations fuel the dreams and aspirations of your sales and service teams; challenge and celebrate your suppliers and vendors; energize your community action or fundraising events; and remind your customers that *your* team is ready and waiting to serve *their* team.

Dan Zadra

ONE PERSON MAY SUPPLY

THE IDEA FOR A COMPANY,

COMMUNITY OR NATION,

BUT WHAT GIVES THE IDEA

ITS FORCE IS A COMMUNITY

OF DREAMS.

— ANDRÉ MALRAUX

We start with the idea that nothing is impossible and everything can be done in the end.
—*Alberta Ferretti*

We are looking for a lot of people who have an infinite capacity to not know what can't be done.
—*Henry Ford*

We have discovered that there are ways of getting almost anywhere we want to go, if we really want to go there.
—*Langston Hughes*

CELEBRATING THE POWER OF A TEAM AND A DREAM.

Impossible is just an opinion.
—*Unknown*

To those who will,
the ways are never wanting.
—*George Herbert*

I have discovered in life that
I can do anything, but I can't
do everything. No one can go
it alone. Create your team!
—*Dr. Robert Schuller*

You alone can do it,
but you can't do it alone.
—*Frank Vizzare*

We may not have it all together,
but together we have it all.
—*Ruth Rogers*

Can't usually means won't.
We can…if we will.
—*Don Ward*

CELEBRATING THE POWER OF A TEAM AND A DREAM.

Don't agonize. Organize.
—*Florynce Kennedy*

It's that simple. I see something worthwhile and important that has to be done and I organize it.
—*Elinore Guggenheimer*

I believe in individuals banding together for a higher purpose. Some people don't like organizations. But it is always awesome to me when you can pool a lot of people who have so many talents. That's when you can really make your program move.
—*Hortense Canady*

Down deep in every human heart is a hidden longing, impulse, and ambition to do something fine and enduring.
—*Grenville Kleiser*

To make a difference is not a matter of accident, a matter of casual occurrence of the tides. People choose to make a difference.
—*Maya Angelou*

The key is to keep company with people who uplift you, whose presence calls forth your best.
—*Epictetus*

CELEBRATING THE POWER OF A TEAM AND A DREAM.

You will find people who want to be
carried on the shoulders of others, who
think that the world owes them a living.
They don't seem to see that we must all
lift together and pull together.

—Henry Ford

Set your expectations high;
find men and women whose
integrity and values you respect; get
their agreement on a course of action;
and give them your ultimate trust.

—John Akers

WE ARE THE ONES WE'VE BEEN WAITING FOR.

—HOPI TEACHING

Sometimes you gotta create
what you want to be a part of.
—*Geri Weitzman*

The world is before you and you
need not take it or leave it as it was
when you came in.
—*James Baldwin*

Your willingness to create
a new dream or vision for
your life is a statement of
belief in your own potential.
—*David McNally*

We all need to believe
in what we are doing.
—*Allan D. Gilmour*

Unhappiness is not
knowing what we want and
killing ourselves to get it.
—*Don Herold*

There are many things in life that will
catch your eye, but only a few will
catch your heart. Pursue these.
—*Unknown*

CELEBRATING THE POWER OF A TEAM AND A DREAM.

The future cannot be predicted, but futures can be invented. It is our ability to invent the future that gives us hope and makes us what we are.
—*Dennis Gabor*

We don't have to take life the way it comes to us. By converting our dreams into goals, and our goals into plans, we can design life to come to us the way we want it. We can live our lives on purpose, instead of by chance.
—*Dan Zadra*

We define ourselves by the
best that is in us, not the worst that
has been done to us.
—*Edward Lewis*

The courage to imagine the otherwise
is our greatest resource, adding color
and suspense to all our life.
—*Daniel Boorstin*

Because where we come from
isn't nearly as important as where
we are going.
—*FareStart*

CELEBRATING THE POWER OF A TEAM AND A DREAM.

Good organizations create
a vision, articulate the vision,
passionately own the vision, and
relentlessly drive it to completion.
—*Jack Welch*

To create a vision, people
have to get beyond their current
inhibitions—they have to dream.
—*Jack Wells*

A vision is not a vision unless it says yes
to some ideas and no to others, inspires
people and is a reason to get out of bed
in the morning and come to work.
—*Gifford Pinchot*

Author Jim Belasco tells the story of Dr. Cooley, the famous brain surgeon. Belasco followed Cooley on his rounds one day and, en route to the operating room, saw the surgeon stop and talk to a man mopping the hallway. They conversed for nearly 10 minutes before Cooley dashed into the operating room. His curiosity raised, Belasco commented, "That was a long conversation." The man mopping the floor replied, "Dr. Cooley talks to me quite often." The author asked, "What do you do at the hospital?" The man replied, "We save lives."

—*"Building Community"*

CELEBRATING THE POWER OF A TEAM AND A DREAM.

The only thing that matters is the bottom
line? What a presumptuous thing to say.
The bottom line's in heaven. The real
business of business is building things.
—*Edwin Land*

Every organization wants to grow.
But tomorrow, who will really care
how fast you grew? Isn't it more
important to know what you are
building with your growth, and why?
—*Brad Saathoff*

Making a living is only part of life.
—*Cecil Andrus*

We work to become,
not to acquire.
—*Elbert Hubbard*

We are more, much more,
than what we have.
—*Don Wilson*

CELEBRATING THE POWER OF A TEAM AND A DREAM.

Living with purpose is more a
question of what we put in
than what we take out.
—*Howard Barnes*

Dreams come true; without
that possibility, nature would
not incite us to have them.
—*John Updike*

If we have a big enough "why,"
we will always discover the "how."
—*Unknown*

THE FUTURE?

THE THINGS THAT

GOT US HERE WILL NOT

GET US THERE.

—PETER DRUCKER

There is nothing stable in the world;
uproar's your only music.
—*John Keats*

Yesterday's answer has nothing
to do with today's problem.
—*Bill Gates*

Part of the economy dies every day
and is replaced by something new.
—*Paul Hawken*

Reorganization is the permanent
condition of a healthy organization.
—*Roy Ash*

Every organization has to
prepare for the abandonment
of everything it does.
—*Peter Drucker*

I am convinced that if the rate of
change inside an organization is less
than the rate of change outside,
the end is in sight.
—*Jack Welch*

CELEBRATING THE POWER OF A TEAM AND A DREAM.

The only person who
likes change is a wet baby.
—*Roy Blitzer*

Faced with the choice between
changing one's mind and proving
that there is no need to do so, almost
everybody gets busy on the proof.
—*John Kenneth Galbraith*

So much has been written about
people's resistance to change that we
are sometimes tempted to forget that
they can also react favorably.
—*Nathaniel Stewart*

People don't dislike change.
They dislike being changed.
—*Mike Basch*

People tend to resist that which
is forced upon them. People tend to
support that which they help to create.
—*Vince Pfaff*

The most effective and enjoyable
way for most of us to cope with
change is to help create it.
—*Unknown*

CELEBRATING THE POWER OF A TEAM AND A DREAM.

The things we fear most in organizations—
disruptions, confusion, chaos—need not
be interpreted as signs that we are about
to be destroyed. Instead, these conditions
are necessary to awaken creativity.
—*Margaret J. Wheatley*

I have a great belief in
the fact that whenever there
is chaos, it creates wonderful
thinking. I consider chaos a gift.
—*Septima Poinsetta Clark*

Change cannot be avoided.
Change provides the opportunity for
innovation. It gives us the chance
to demonstrate our creativity.
—*Keshavan Nair*

It takes a lot of courage to release
the familiar and seemingly secure, to
embrace the new. But there is no real
security in what is no longer meaningful.
There is more security in the adventurous
and exciting, for in movement there is
life and in change there is power.
—*Alan Cohen*

CELEBRATING THE POWER OF A TEAM AND A DREAM.

We don't have an eternity to realize
our dreams, only the time we are here.
—*Susan Taylor*

We cannot become what we
want to be by remaining what we are.
—*Max DePree*

Are we willing to give up some things
we like to do, in order to move on to
those things we must do?
—*Satenig St. Marie*

Tradition is our guide,
not a jailer.
—*W. Somerset Maugham*

Change is inevitable.
It's direction that counts.
—*Gil Atkinson*

Be willing to change anything and
everything, including your mind.
The only sacred cow is your principles.
—*Buck Rodgers*

CELEBRATING THE POWER OF A TEAM AND A DREAM.

TOGETHER
WE CAN

Open your arms to change,
but don't let go of your values.
—*Unknown*

An organization's values
are its life's blood.
—*Max DePree*

The main dangers in this life are
the people who want to change
everything--or nothing.
—*Lady Nancy Astor*

A company or a team needs to be constantly rejuvenated by the infusion of young blood. It needs young people with the imagination and the guts to turn everything upside down if they can. It also needs old fogies to keep them from turning upside down those things that ought to be right side up. Above all, it needs young rebels and old conservatives who can work together, challenge each other's values, yield or hold fast with equal grace, and continue after each hard-fought battle to respect each other.

—*"Building Community"*

CELEBRATING THE POWER OF A TEAM AND A DREAM.

Ideas bring people together,
but ideals hold them together.
—*Dan Zadra*

Superior work teams recognize that
consistently high performance can be
built not on rules, but only on values.
—*Dennis Kinlaw*

We will compromise on almost anything,
but not on our values, or our aesthetics,
or our idealism, or our sense of curiosity.
—*Anita Roddick*

TRUST YOUR

CRAZY IDEAS.

—DAN ZADRA

The next time your mind wanders,
follow it around for awhile.
—*Jessica Masterson*

Not all those that
wander are lost.
—*J.R.R. Tolkien*

Discoveries are often made by
not following instructions, by going off
the main road, by trying the untried.
—*Frank Tyger*

Blessed are the curious
for they shall have adventures.
—*Lovelle Drachman*

We just keep moving forward, opening
new doors, and doing new things,
because we're curious and curiosity
keeps leading us down new paths.
—*Walt Disney*

Don't be confined by reality or precedent.
Think about what could be accomplished
if there were no boundaries.
—*James Fantus*

CELEBRATING THE POWER OF A TEAM AND A DREAM.

Take out your brain and
jump on it—it gets all caked up.
—*Unknown*

Your brain is a vast database of
30 billion neurons, each storing up to
a million bits of information. Let new
data and experiences bounce freely
in your mind like a pinball. You'll rack
up countless new connections;
some will be real breakthroughs.
—*Dan Zadra*

Creativity is like a muscle.
You either use it or lose it.
—*Roger von Oech*

Innovation is simply
group intelligence having fun.
—*Michael Nolan*

Creativity is inventing, experimenting,
growing, taking risks, breaking rules,
making mistakes and having fun.
—*Mary Lou Cook*

They trashed the rules and found
new ways to win.
—*Mark Roman*

CELEBRATING THE POWER OF A TEAM AND A DREAM.

New ideas are not born
in a conforming environment.
—*Roger von Oech*

Don't expect anything original
from an echo.
—*Unknown*

People will accept your ideas
much more readily if you tell them
Benjamin Franklin said it first.
—*David H. Comins*

40

If you have always done it that way,
it is probably wrong.
—*Charles F. Kettering*

Chances are the more
puzzled looks your idea creates,
the better your idea is.
—*United Technologies*

Big ideas are so hard to recognize, so
fragile, so easy to kill. Don't forget that,
all of you who don't have them.
—*John Elliott, Jr.*

CELEBRATING THE POWER OF A TEAM AND A DREAM.

You have a creative
contribution to make. Your life,
and mine, will be better if you do.
—*Michael Toms*

Every organization needs
torchbearers. These are the people
who discover new ideas, systems
or innovations and champion the
charge to have them implemented.
—*"Bits & Pieces"*

There is no such thing as
continuous improvement without
continuous innovation.
—*Don Galer*

It first appeared like a crazy idea.
It turned out he had a great idea.
—*J. Richard Munro*

Like all revolutionary new ideas, the subject has had to pass through three stages, which may be summed up by three reactions: 1) "It's crazy—don't waste my time." 2) "It's possible, but it's not worth doing." 3) "I always said it was a good idea."
—*Arthur C. Clarke*

CELEBRATING THE POWER OF A TEAM AND A DREAM.

TOGETHER
WE CAN

Trade minds with each other.
Ideas build on ideas.
One idea leads to another.
—Don Ward

I start where the last person left off.
—Thomas Edison

A single idea can transform a life,
a business, a nation, a world.
—Dan Zadra

44

There is no doubt about it—
ideas change history.
—*Frank Goble*

Invention breeds invention.
The tea kettle led Fulton to the primitive
steam engine, which led to the gas
combustion engine, which led to the
modern rocket propulsion system—
which took us to the moon and back.
—*Dan Zadra*

Anything can happen.
That's the beauty of creating.
—*Ernie Harwell*

CELEBRATING THE POWER OF A TEAM AND A DREAM.

I believe that the creativity that twisted
a piece of wire into a paperclip…
is great enough to create brotherhood
and universal peace.
—*Wilfred Peterson*

What we have done has barely
scratched the surface. It turns out that
there is, in fact, unlimited juice in that
lemon. The fact is that none of this is
about squeezing anything at all—it is
about tapping an ocean of creativity,
passion and energy that, as far as we
can see, has no bottom and no shores.
—*Jack Welch*

46

IF WE DON'T

EXECUTE OUR IDEAS,

THEY'LL DIE.

—ROBERT PERCIVAL

Ideas are one thing and
what happens is another.
—*John Cage*

Anybody can come up with new ideas.
Innovators make them happen.
—*Michael LeBoeuf*

Unless commitment is made,
there are only promises and
hopes, but no plan.
—*Peter Drucker*

It's the start that stops most people.
—*Phil Rognier*

We are always afraid to start something that we want to make very good, true and serious.
—*Brenda Ueland*

The "what if?" question begs for completion: "What if we tried?"
—*Dale Dauten*

CELEBRATING THE POWER OF A TEAM AND A DREAM.

Nothing will ever be attempted,
if all possible objections
must first be overcome.
—*Samuel Johnson*

You'll never have all the
information you need to make a
decision—if you did, it would be a
foregone conclusion, not a decision.
—*David Mahoney, Jr.*

We have forty million reasons for
failure, but not a single excuse.
—*Rudyard Kipling*

SOME WORN-OUT REASONS: NEVER DONE IT BEFORE.
NEVER BEEN TRIED BEFORE. WE TRIED IT BEFORE. WE'VE
BEEN DOING IT THIS WAY FOR YEARS. IT WON'T WORK IN
A SMALL (LARGE) COMPANY. IT WON'T WORK IN OUR
COMPANY. WHY CHANGE—IT'S WORKING OKAY.
THE BOSS WILL NEVER BUY IT. NEEDS FURTHER STUDY.
TOO MUCH TROUBLE. WE'RE DIFFERENT. AD DEPT. SAYS
IT CAN'T BE DONE. SALES DEPT. SAYS IT CAN'T BE SOLD.
SERVICE DEPT. WON'T LIKE IT. DON'T HAVE THE MONEY,
PERSONNEL, EQUIPMENT, TIME. IT'S NOT MY JOB. IT WILL
INCREASE OVERHEAD. EMPLOYEES WILL NEVER BUY INTO IT.
IT'S NOT OUR PROBLEM. YOU'RE RIGHT, BUT…WE'RE NOT
READY FOR IT. WE CAN'T TAKE THE CHANCE. WE'D LOSE
MONEY ON IT. IT TAKES TOO LONG TO PAY OUT.
NEEDS SLEEPING ON. IT'S IMPOSSIBLE.

—E. F. BORISCH

It is the business of
the future to be dangerous.
—*Alfred North Whitehead*

It is not given us to live lives
of undisrupted calm, boredom,
and mediocrity. It is given us
to be edge-dwellers.
—*Jay Deacon*

Everyone in a successful organization
must be willing to risk. Risk is like
change; it's not a choice.
—*Max DePree*

Growth demands a
temporary surrender of security.
—*Gail Sheehy*

Why be afraid of something we want?
—*Erin Mosley*

So what do we do?
Anything. Something. So long
as we just don't sit there. If we screw
it up, start over. Try something else.
If we wait until we've satisfied all the
uncertainties, it may be too late.
—*Lee Iacocca*

The freedom to fail is vital if
you're going to succeed.
—*Michael Korda*

We don't grow unless
we take risks. Any successful
company is riddled with failures.
—*James E. Burke*

The only people who never fail
are those who never try.
—*Ilka Chase*

Someday is not a day of the week.
—*Unknown*

Don't let the possibilities be suffocated
by procrastination. Go! Now!
—*Dr. Robert Schuller*

Inertia is the only menace.
—*Saint-John Perse*

We never know how high we are
till we are called to rise.
—*Emily Dickinson*

You can do anything in
this world if you are prepared
to take the consequences.
—*W. Somerset Maugham*

All of us can take steps—no matter how
small and insignificant at the start—
in the direction we want to go.
—*Marsha Sinetar*

Be assured that any worthwhile action
will create change and attract support.
—*Philip Marvin*

Opportunities multiply as
they are seized.
—*Sun Tzu*

The simple act of commitment is a
powerful magnet for help. The moment
we commit and quit holding back, all
sorts of unforeseen people, events and
circumstances will rise up to assist us.
—*Napolean Hill*

CELEBRATING THE POWER OF A TEAM AND A DREAM.

Most of my ideas belonged to
other people who didn't bother
to develop them.
—Thomas Edison

I wonder what becomes of lost
opportunities. Perhaps our guardian angel
gathers them up as we drop them, and
will give them back to us in the beautiful
sometime when we have grown wiser, and
learned how to use them rightly.
—Helen Keller

RESIGN AS

GENERAL MANAGER

OF THE UNIVERSE—AND

TRUST YOUR TEAM.

—LARRY EISENBERG

There is greatness all around you—
welcome it! It is easy to be great
when you get around great people.
—*Bob Richards*

Teamwork has its own arithmetic.
Combine two or more people with
a common goal and suddenly
one-plus-one is more than two.
—*Dan Zadra*

Snowflakes are a fragile thing
individually, but look at what they
can do when they stick together.
—*Fernando Bonaventura*

Each of us, individually, walks with
the tread of a fox, but collectively
we fly as the geese!
—*Solon*

Remember the law of accumulation:
The sum of many little collaborative
efforts isn't little.
—*Dan Zadra*

The whole is the sum of its parts.
Be a good part.
—*Nate McConnell*

CELEBRATING THE POWER OF A TEAM AND A DREAM.

Ask your team—
they know the answer.
—Chuck Carlson

There is somebody smarter than
any of us, and that is all of us.
—Michael Nolan

There are precious few
Einsteins among us. Most brilliance arises
from ordinary people working
together in extraordinary ways.
—Roger von Oech

It takes each of us
to make a difference for all of us.
—*Jackie Mutcheson*

No one can be the best at
everything. But when all of us
combine our talents, we can and will
be the best at virtually anything.
—*Dan Zadra*

Those who are not team players
will have to go.
—*Jeanne Greenberg*

CELEBRATING THE POWER OF A TEAM AND A DREAM.

We have to be able to
count on each other doing
what we have agreed to do.
—*Phil Crosby*

If I can count on you, and you
can count on me, just think what
a wonderful world this will be.
—*Childhood rhyme*

Trust each other again and again.
When the trust level gets high enough,
people transcend apparent limitations
and discover new and awesome abilities
that were previously unapparent.
—*David Armistead*

The secret of stardom
is the rest of the team.
—*John Wooden*

As a coach, I play not my
eleven best, but my best eleven.
—*Knute Rockne*

The team player knows that it doesn't
matter who gets the credit as long as
the job gets done. If the job gets done,
the credit will come.
—*The EDGE*

CELEBRATING THE POWER OF A TEAM AND A DREAM.

LEADERSHIP IS ACTION,

NOT POSITION.

—DONALD H. McGANNON

I've had it with organizations that are afraid to let their people do things.
—*Al Grey*

We have to undo a 100-year-old concept and convince our managers that their role is not to control people and stay "on top" of things, but rather to guide, energize and excite.
—*Jack Welch*

You gave me wings, now let me fly.
—*Don Ward*

CELEBRATING THE POWER OF A TEAM AND A DREAM.

Never tell people how to do things.
Tell them what to do and they will
surprise you with their ingenuity.
—General George Patton

The entire Policies and Procedures
manual for Nordstrom personnel:
"Use your best judgment at all times."
—"Commitment To Excellence"

Hire the best. Pay them fairly.
Communicate frequently. Provide
meaningful challenges and rewards.
Believe in them. Trust them. Get out of
their way—they'll knock your socks off!
—Mary Ann Allison

People don't want to be managed. They want to be led. Whoever heard of a world manager? World leader, yes. Educational leader. Political leader. Religious leader. Community leader. Labor leader. Business leader. They lead; they don't manage. Ask your horse. You can lead your horse to water, but you can't manage him to drink. If you want to manage somebody, manage yourself. Do that well and you'll be ready to stop managing. And start leading.

—*United Technologies*

CELEBRATING THE POWER OF A TEAM AND A DREAM.

The humility which comes with
others having faith in you....
—*Dag Hammarskjöld*

The first responsibility of the leader
is to define what can be. The last is
to say thank you. In between the
two, the leader must become
a servant and a debtor.
—*Max DePree*

Being a leader is not about making
yourself more powerful. It's about making
people around you more powerful.
—*Betty Linton*

Morale is self-esteem in action.
—*Avery Weisman, M.D.*

The aim of the great leader is not to get people to think more highly of the leader. It's to get people to think more highly of themselves.
—*EDGE Learning*

It's not who we are that holds us back, it's who we think we're not.
—*Michael Nolan*

CELEBRATING THE POWER OF A TEAM AND A DREAM.

If you want someone to do a good job,
give them a good job to do.
—*Frederick Herzberg*

If he works for you, you work for him.
—*Japanese proverb*

I don't believe in just ordering
people to do things. You have to sort
of grab an oar and row with them.
—*Harold Geneen*

"Do-so" is more important than "say-so."
—*Pete Seeger*

Strange as it sounds, great leaders gain
authority by giving it away.
—*James B. Stockdale*

It is commitment, not authority,
that produces results.
—*William Gore*

Love people; use things.
Not vice versa.
—*Kelly Ann Rothaus*

I use the business to make
great people. I don't use people
to make a great business.
—*Ralph Stayer*

In the end, the leader casts
a long shadow. What kind of
a shadow are you casting?
—*James Belasco*

WE ARE DROWNING IN

INFORMATION WHILE

STARVING FOR WISDOM.

— E.O. WILSON

The one thing that must not be
withheld from people who live and
work in the Information Age
is information.
—*Vince Pfaff*

Communication loves a vacuum.
—*Dan Zadra*

If you don't provide your
teammates with information, they'll
make up something to fill the void.
—*Carla O'Dell*

76

Bricks and mortar don't
ask why. But people do, and
people deserve answers.
—*John Guaspari*

An individual without information
cannot take responsibility; an individual
who is given information cannot help
but take responsibility.
—*Jan Carlzon*

Innovation comes only from readily
and seamlessly sharing information
rather than hoarding it.
—*Tom Peters*

CELEBRATING THE POWER OF A TEAM AND A DREAM.

There is a profound difference
between information and meaning.
—*Warren Bennis*

Everything is data.
But data isn't everything.
—*Pauline Bart*

Where is the wisdom we have lost in
knowledge? Where is the knowledge
we have lost in information?
—*T.S. Eliot*

Feedback is the
breakfast of champions.
—*Ken Blanchard*

No one wants advice,
we want collaboration.
—*Rian Jones*

The two words "information" and
"communication" are often used
interchangeably, but they signify quite
different things. Information is giving
out; communication is getting through.
—*Sydney J. Harris*

CELEBRATING THE POWER OF A TEAM AND A DREAM.

Be careful, think about the effect of what you say. Your words should be constructive, bring people together, not pull them apart.
—*Miriam Makeba*

The word "communication" comes from the same Latin root as the word "communion." It literally means "to come together." If what we say isn't helping us come together—with our friends, our family, our colleagues, our community—then chances are it's not communication, it's something else.
—*Dan Zadra*

CARING IS

A POWERFUL BUSINESS

ADVANTAGE.

—SCOTT JOHNSON

Draw strength from each other.
—*James A. Renier*

The success or failure of any company
boils down to one question: Are you
operating from passion? If you are,
you're going to succeed. If you believe
in what you're doing, you're going
to make sure everyone around you
believes in it too.
—*Maggie Hughes*

Each of us has a spark of life inside us,
and our highest endeavor ought to be
to set off that spark in one another.
—*Kenny Ausubel*

What have you done
for your team today?
—*William Platt*

When the term "community" is used,
the notion that typically comes to
mind is a place in which people know
and care for one another—the kind of
place in which people do not merely
ask "How are you?" as a formality, but
care about the answer.
—*Amitai Etzioni*

It all boils down to those who really
care, and those who really don't.
—*Dan Zadra*

CELEBRATING THE POWER OF A TEAM AND A DREAM.

Nobody notices when things go right.
—Zimmerman's Law of Complaints

There seems to be an automatic
assumption that negative is realistic
and positive is unrealistic.
—Susan Jeffers

Tell the negative committee that meets
in your head to sit down and shut up.
—Kathy Kendall

Don't overreact to the
grumblers and troublemakers.
—*Beth Bingham*

Remember that one-fifth
of the people are against
everything all the time.
—*Robert Kennedy*

Let the ideas clash but not the hearts.
—*C.C. Mehta*

CELEBRATING THE POWER OF A TEAM AND A DREAM.

Difficulties are meant
to rouse, not discourage.
—*William Ellery Channing*

Problems are the price of progress.
Don't bring me anything but trouble—
good news weakens me.
—*Charles F. Kettering*

Problems can become opportunities
when the right people come together.
—*Robert Redford*

Where others see problems,
we can see possibilities.
—*Diane Dreher*

Let's all strategize how the job can
get done, versus informing each other
why it can't be done.
—*Melissa Gonzales*

Help each other be right, not wrong.
Look for ways to make new ideas work,
not for reasons they won't. Do everything
with enthusiasm, it's contagious.
—*Ian Percy*

CELEBRATING THE POWER OF A TEAM AND A DREAM.

Excellence is not a spectator
sport. Everyone's involved.
—*Jack Welch*

Most of us never qualify for life's
grand awards—no Oscar, Emmy
or Nobel Prize. But we all have a
shot at one worthwhile pursuit—
the chance to deliver quality in
all that we do for others.
—*Dan Zadra*

Don't just create what
the market needs or wants.
Create what it would love.
—*Josh Armstrong*

Beautiful things make money.
—*Geoffrey Beene*

The average American salesperson
keeps 33 men and women at work—
33 people producing the product he
or she sells—and is responsible for the
livelihood of 130 people.
—*Robert Whitney*

Our checks that go to our people say,
"From our customers," because we want
to remind everyone that it's not some
addition to the general office that
produces that check; it's the customers.
—*Herb Kelleher*

CELEBRATING THE POWER OF A TEAM AND A DREAM.

Quality is not any single thing but an aura, an atmosphere, an overpowering feeling that a company is doing everything with excellence.
—*Jack Welch*

Service is not just a noun, it's a verb. It's not just a job, it's a calling. It's not just a way of doing business, it's a philosophy of life.
—*Don Ward*

If you believe in unlimited quality, and act in all your business dealings with total integrity, the rest will take care of itself.
—*Frank Perdue*

WE ARE, OF COURSE,

A NATION OF DIFFERENCES.

THOSE DIFFERENCES DON'T

MAKE US WEAK, THEY'RE THE

SOURCE OF OUR STRENGTH.

—JIMMY CARTER

The most universal quality is diversity.
—*Michel de Montaigne*

We are all unique, and if that
is not fulfilled, then something
wonderful has been lost.
—*Martha Graham*

I note the obvious differences between
each sort and type, but we are more
alike, my friends, than we are unalike.
—*Maya Angelou*

There is no such thing as "them and us."
In a world this size there can only be
"we"—all of us working together.
—*Don Ward*

The best hope of solving all
our problems lies in harnessing
the diversity, the energy and the
creativity of all our people.
—*Roger Wilkins*

Either we're pulling together or
we're pulling apart. There's really
no in-between.
—*Kobi Yamada*

CELEBRATING THE POWER OF A TEAM AND A DREAM.

Herald the day when we can
always appreciate each other.
—*Des'ree*

Let us begin to see the true promise of
our country and community, not as a
melting pot, but as a kaleidoscope.
—*Robert Kennedy*

The great organizations celebrate the
differences. They seek harmony, not
uniformity. They hire talent, not color.
They strive for oneness, not sameness.
—*Gil Atkinson*

Some people think that
seeking diversity automatically
leads to excellence, but I think
focusing on excellence inevitably
leads to diversity.
—*William C. Steere*

Understanding and accepting diversity
enables us to see that each of us is
needed. It also enables us to begin to
think about being abandoned to the
strengths of others, of admitting that we
cannot know or do everything.
—*Max DePree*

CELEBRATING THE POWER OF A TEAM AND A DREAM.

Diversity: The art of thinking
independently together.
—*Malcolm Forbes*

To see brotherhood in action, just watch
a bunch of high-school kids taking a final
exam. There's no question of race, creed,
gender or color. There is only one question:
"Who's got the answer?"
—*Sam Levenson*

Brilliance comes in all colors,
strengths in many forms. When we
learn to honor the differences and
appreciate the mix, we're on our way!
—*Kelly Ann Rothaus*

96

SUCCESS IS

SWEETEST WHEN IT'S

SHARED.

—HOWARD SCHULTZ

People come together because they
need each other, and they also need
to hear victories about each other.
—Bill Milliken

When people act heroically,
treat them as heroes.
—Jeff Goforth

When someone does something
good, applaud! You will make
two people happy.
—Samuel Goldwyn

Celebrate what
you want to see more of!
—*Tom Peters*

The deepest principle in human nature
is the craving to be appreciated.
—*William James*

Everyone who does the best he or
she can do should be considered a
hero. The five most important words:
"You did a great job."
—*Anonymous*

CELEBRATING THE POWER OF A TEAM AND A DREAM.

Failures are few among
people who have found a work
they enjoy enough to do it well.
—-*Clarence Flynn*

People are always good
company when they are doing
what they really enjoy.
—*Samuel Butler*

To love what you do and
feel that it matters—-how could
anything be more fun?
—*Katharine Graham*

Experiencing the silent satisfaction of a job well done. Fulfilling high expectations for customers. Sharing and celebrating team victories. Making the most of our time together and anticipating an even brighter future. Knowing in our hearts that even our most routine tasks make a meaningful contribution to our company Vision, and therefore to the world—this makes the difference between eight hours of "have to" and eight hours of "want to." This makes work fun.

—LensCrafters

CELEBRATING THE POWER OF A TEAM AND A DREAM.

I passionately beseech each and every
one of you to stamp out bureaucracy
wherever you encounter it, especially in
your own team or organization.
—*Frank Vizzare*

The perfect bureaucrat...
manages to make no decisions
and escape all responsibility.
—*Brooks Atkinson*

Bureaucracy is nothing more than a
hardening of an organization's arteries.
—*William Anthony*

102

If you're working in an organization that is NOT enthusiastic, energetic, creative, clever, curious, and just plain fun, you've got troubles… serious troubles.
—*Tom Peters*

Is not life a hundred times too short for us to bore ourselves?
—*Friedrich Nietzsche*

We can't sweep other people off their feet if we can't be swept off our own.
—*Clarence Day*

CELEBRATING THE POWER OF A TEAM AND A DREAM.

No plan emerges unscathed
from its collision with reality.
—Shirley Abbott

All have disappointments, all have
times when it isn't worthwile.
—John H. Hanson

Most of the important things in the
world have been accomplished by
people who have kept on trying when
there seemed to be no hope at all.
—Dale Carnegie

I had to pick myself up and
get on with it, do it all over again,
only even better this time.
—*Sam Walton*

It's supposed to be hard; if it
wasn't hard, everyone would do it.
The hard is what makes it great.
—*Tom Hanks in "A League of Her Own"*

There is nothing we cannot live down,
rise above and overcome.
—*Ella Wheeler Wilcox*

CELEBRATING THE POWER OF A TEAM AND A DREAM.

I thank God that I live in a country where dreams can come true, where failure is the first step to success, and where success is only another form of failure if we forget what our priorities should be.
—*Harry Lloyd*

If you defy the system long enough you'll be rewarded. At first life takes revenge and reduces you to a sniveling mess. But keep sniveling, have the madness, the audacity, to do what interests you, keep faith with your team, and eventually life will say, all right, we'll let you do it.
—*Jo Coudert*

WE SHOULD ALL BE

CONCERNED ABOUT THE FUTURE

BECAUSE WE WILL HAVE TO SPEND

THE REST OF OUR LIVES THERE.

—CHARLES F. KETTERING

The future is of our own making—and
the most striking characteristic of the
century is just that development.
—*Joseph Conrad*

In every community, there is work
to be done. In every nation, there
are wounds to heal. In every heart,
there is the power to do it.
—*Marianne Williamson*

There is nothing wrong with
America that cannot be cured by
what's right with the America.
—*Bill Clinton*

Never doubt that a small group of thoughtful, committed people can change the world; indeed, it is the only thing that ever has.
—*Margaret Mead*

I have always believed I could help change the world, because I have been lucky to have adults around me who actually did.
—*Marian Wright Edelman*

CELEBRATING THE POWER OF A TEAM AND A DREAM.

People say, "What is the sense of our small efforts?" They cannot see that we must lay one brick at a time, take one step at a time.
—*Dorothy Day*

If you don't like the way the world is, you change it. You have an obligation to change it.
—*Marian Wright Edelman*

To live in society doesn't mean simply living side by side with others in a more or less close cohesion; it means living through one another and for one another.
—*Paul-Eugène Roy*

Start where you are.
Distant fields always look greener,
but opportunity lies right where
you are. Take advantage of every
opportunity of service.
—*Robert Collier*

This is a wonderful country. This is a
great place. Sometimes we don't see it.
But I encourage people to look a little
bit harder because if we look with our
hearts, if we look with hope, we will find
a people and a country and a world
worth living in.
—*Ron Kovic*

CELEBRATING THE POWER OF A TEAM AND A DREAM.

Our country is not made up
of stocks or bonds or gold—it is
comprised of the hopes and
dreams in our minds and hearts.
—*Unknown*

Despite our success, we are not a
selfish people. On the frontier, people
got together to raise a neighbor's barn.
Today, people all across the country
·raise something just as important—
billions of dollars per year in charitable
donations and volunteer services.
—*Don Dougherty*

This country is generous, giving, compassionate and sacrificing. Many millions contribute to the United Way, drive ambulances, fight fires, save lives, help the disadvantaged, contribute to medical research, serve in the armed forces, encourage youth, dance with the elderly and comfort the sick. If you're one of the above, you ain't what's wrong with this country.
—*Grey Matter*

People who develop the habit of thinking of themselves as world citizens are fulfilling the first requirement of sanity in our time.
—*Norman Cousins*

CELEBRATING THE POWER OF A TEAM AND A DREAM.

The greatest challenge of the day is:
How to bring about a revolution of the
heart, a revolution that has to start
with each one of us?
—*Dorothy Day*

Few will have the greatness to bend
history itself; but each of us can work
to change a small portion of events,
and in the total of all those acts will be
written the history of this generation.
—*Robert Kennedy*

What can you do to promote world peace? Go home and love your family.
—*Mother Teresa*

I think that the most significant work we will ever do, is in the four walls of our own home.
—*Stephen R. Covey, Ph.D.*

Let us take care of the children, for they have a long way to go. Let us take care of the elders, for they have come a long way. Let us take care of those in between, for they are doing the work.
—*African prayer*

CELEBRATING THE POWER OF A TEAM AND A DREAM.

Mankind has advanced in the
footsteps of men and women of
unshakable faith. Many of these great
ones have set stars in the heavens
to light others through the night.
—*Olga Rosmanith*

What was most significant about the lunar
voyage was not that men set foot on the
Moon, but that they set eye on the Earth.
—*Norman Cousins*

We may well go to the moon, but that's
not very far. The greatest distance
we have to cover still lies within us.
—*Charles de Gaulle*

If we want to make something really superb of this planet, there is nothing whatever that can stop us.
—*Shepherd Mead*

Some people give time, some money, some their skills and connections, some literally give their life's blood… but everyone has something to give.
—*Barbara Bush*

To the world you may be just one person, but to one person you may be the world.
—*Josephine Billings*

CELEBRATING THE POWER OF A TEAM AND A DREAM.

BUT A GREATER

THING IS TO FIGHT LIFE

THROUGH, AND AT THE END,

"THE DREAM IS TRUE!"

—EDWIN MARKHAM

The world ages us too fast. We grow up too quickly, we stop dreaming too early, and we develop the ability to worry at far too young an age.
—*Doug Wecker*

People say life is so short. That isn't true at all. Life is so long that we don't have a moment to waste without forgiveness and loving kindness. Life is so long that many people have died years before they actually reached their deathbed.
—*Deepak Chopra, M.D.*

Some people succumb to cynicism.
They lose their zest for life too early
and really could have this as their
epitaph: *Died at 40, buried at 80.*
—Bob Moawad

Don't lose faith in humanity. Think of
all the people in the world who have
never played you a single nasty trick.
—Elbert Hubbard

Let your friends, colleagues and family
know about the good that you see;
it will help them see it too.
—Hanoch McCarty

Our obligation is to give meaning
to life and in doing so to overcome
the passive, indifferent life.
—*Elie Wiesel*

The only real aging process
is the erosion of our ideals.
—*Albert Schweitzer*

Start now. Leave a timeless
legacy. Plant trees. Grow people.
Your finest hour is yet to be.
—*James Belasco*

CELEBRATING THE POWER OF A TEAM AND A DREAM.

Think beyond your lifetime if
you want to accomplish something
truly worthwhile.
—*Walt Disney*

Someone's sitting in the shade
today because someone planted
a tree a long time ago.
—*Warren Buffett*

The influence of each human being on
others in this life is a kind of immortality.
—*John Quincy Adams*

122

Whatever has crowded out the individual's growth needs to be recognized and removed.
—*Jean Shinoda Bolen*

I am delighted to find that even at my great age, ideas come to me, the pursuit of which would require a second life.
—*Johann von Goethe*

The questions asked at the end of our lives are very simple: "Did we love well? Did we love our community, the earth, in a deep way?" And perhaps, "Did we live fully? Did we offer ourselves to life?"
—*Jack Kornfield*

CELEBRATING THE POWER OF A TEAM AND A DREAM.

I'm going to tap dance until I can't.
—*Gregory Hines*

If you're putting off something you've been meaning to do, what are you waiting for? Always wanted to play the banjo? Start taking lessons. Dream about visiting the Greek Islands? Call a travel agent. Hate your bathroom wall paper? Scrape it off and paint. Love the taste of home-grown tomatoes? Plant your own. Angry about the potholes in your street? Go to your town meetings. Whatever you've been putting off, do it now. Tomorrow may be too late.
—*Grey Matter*

Where there is an open mind
there will always be a frontier.
—*Charles F. Kettering*

A frontier is never a place; it is a time
and a way of life. Frontiers pass, but
they endure in their people.
—*Hal Borland*

The New Frontier of which I speak is not a
set of promises—it is a set of challenges.
It sums up not what is offered to you, but
what is asked of you.
—*John F. Kennedy*

CELEBRATING THE POWER OF A TEAM AND A DREAM.

Advice late in life from my father:
"Do more, go farther, reach higher than
me, and pass it on to your children."
—*James Belasco*

It is not impossibilities that fill us with
the deepest despair, but possibilities
which we have failed to realize.
—*Robert Mallet*

Twenty years from now you will be
more disappointed by the things you
didn't do than by the ones you did do.
So throw off the bowlines. Sail away from
the safe harbor. Catch the trade winds
in your sails. Explore. Dream. Discover.
—*Mark Twain*

YOU ASK ME HOW I WANT

TO BE REMEMBERED, WHAT I

WANT ON MY TOMBSTONE?

"SI SE PUEDE—IT CAN BE DONE!"

—DOLORES HUERTA

Other "Gift of Inspiration" books available:

Be Happy
Remember to live, love,
laugh and learn

Be the Difference

Because of You
Celebrating the Difference You Make

Brilliance
Uncommon voices from
uncommon women

Commitment to Excellence
Celebrating the Very Best

Diversity
Celebrating the Differences

Everyone Leads
It takes each of us to make
a difference for all of us

Expect Success
Our Commitment to Our Customer

Forever Remembered
A Gift for the Grieving Heart

I Believe in You
To your heart, your dream,
and the difference you make

Little Miracles
Cherished messages of hope,
joy, love, kindness and courage

Reach for the Stars
Give up the good to go for the great

Team Works
Working Together Works

Thank You
In appreciation of you,
and all that you do

To Your Success
Thoughts to Give Wings to
Your Work and Your Dreams

Welcome Home
Celebrating the Best
Place on Earth

What's Next
Creating the Future Now

Whatever It Takes
A Journey into the Heart
of Human Achievement

You've Got a Friend
Thoughts to Celebrate the
Joy of Friendship